1994 Edition
Published by Wishing Well Books,
an imprint of Joshua Morris Publishing, Inc.,
221 Danbury Road, Wilton, CT 06897.
Copyright © 1986 The Five Mile Press Pty. Ltd.
All rights reserved. Printed in Singapore.
ISBN: 0-88705-750-0
10 9 8 7 6 5 4 3 2 1

Daisy's Wild Ride

BOB GRAHAM

WISHING WELL BOOKS™

Here is Jane with her
cart and her pig, Daisy.

Jane pushes her cart.
This makes it move.

Off they go!

Whee . . . down the hill.

The cart is moving fast.

So is Daisy.

Will they ever stop?

The cart keeps moving until . . .

. . . a rock stops the cart.
But Daisy is still moving.

What will stop Daisy?

Daisy slides into a muddy puddle.

The sticky mud stops Daisy.
Pigs love mud.

You can start a cart moving
with a push.

Once it is moving . . .

it keeps on moving . . .

. . . until it stops.

moving

Moving objects come to rest, even when no apparent force is applied, because of the forces exerted by gravity and friction. Gravity is the force of attraction that pulls objects toward the center of the earth. Friction is the resistance between two surfaces that are moving against one another. Friction can be reduced by using smooth surfaces and/or by providing a lubricant.

Experiments to try

1. Have your child run a metal zipper quickly up and down to gauge the drag caused by friction, and then carefully run the tip of a pencil along the closed zipper track. Do this a number of times. Now have your child try the zipper again. What happens? Why? (The graphite in pencils is a lubricant.)

2. Place a brick on a flat concrete area. Have your child push the brick—without jerking it— along the ground to gauge the force required to move it. Now place two or three rollers between the brick and the concrete. (Pencils or dowels will do.) Have your child push the brick again. What happens?